T0158877

Palsy
I Am Not

Palsy
I Am Not

TERRELL SCOTT

PALSY I AM NOT

iUniverse books may be ordered through booksellers or by contacting:

iUniverse
1663 Liberty Drive
Bloomington, IN 47403
www.iuniverse.com
1-800-Authors (1-800-288-4677)

ISBN: 978-1-5320-0324-0 (sc)
ISBN: 978-1-5320-0325-7 (e)

Library of Congress Control Number: 2016911981

Print information available on the last page.

iUniverse rev. date: 01/23/2017

INTRODUCTION

My Heart's Desire

My heart's desire is to reach people of all ages, origins, and race. I want to ensure that there is a soul saved through my testimony. My main focus now is to change the hearts and minds of disabled people, and the ones with disabilities. There may be people out there with this disease that is confused about it or is questioning God about it. In this book, you will find how I found clarity, and understanding on how to cope with it, and make a difference no matter who I was. People sometimes hurt us with the words that they say, because they do not have the full knowledge and understanding of this disease. Staying positive with both my attitude and my emotions helps me to stay focus on the plan that God has for my life. I want to help heal every broken thing that has happened in your life with the love of God that I have, and display each and every day. For many years, people who are disabled or have any disability are looked at as their minds are trapped in cages and can't do anything for themselves. Disabled people are not animals nor are they any different than the average person. Disabled people are sometimes limited, they are told what they can, and cannot do. However, I have learned that If you put God first in your life, then there are no limitations to what you can do. The negative behaviors from uneducated people have significantly discouraged many individuals with a disability and have caused them not to want to accomplish and achieve their goals in their lives. As you further read this book, I will point out some things that helped me live my life in the way that God intended me to live. God has given us all a purpose, vision and wisdom to live a productive life in Him. I have found that I must have a spiritual connection with God with the covenant and commitment that I have made with God. It is imperative that you have integrity in the life that you live, believe what you say, and live what you say. You will learn as you further read this book that I have been through whole lots of things, even been let down, or even turned away by people, because of my disability. I turned it all into positives, and I used everything that has hurt me to motivate me to accomplish all of my goals in life. None of us chose the life that we have, but yet we must trust in God through it all.

I never understood why God have allowed me to be with Cerebral Palsy, and I have learned not to question His Authority. Then He revealed to me that I am not Cerebral Palsy. God said He allowed me to be in the form of a disabled person to reach out to the ones who have been hurt used and abused. I have been on drugs since I was a fetus, but I had no idea it was all in the plan of God to get me to this point in my life. The name Palsy came from the mental disorder disease that is caused at birth. Cerebral Palsy is a condition that is considered as a non-progressive brain injury. Cerebral Palsy disables you to have motives skills with muscle complication to the body.

Remember just because you are disabled, you are not stuck, but you can do all things that God has enabled you to do.

ACKNOWLEDGEMENTS

My life has impacted so many people that, I wish I could thank them all, but I do not want to leave anyone out. So to everyone who has ever had some contact with me I want to thank you all for being a part of my life. I first would like to honor our Father Jesus Christ who is the Author and the creator of my life. I dedicate this book to him.

I would like to thank all of my supporters throughout the process. Author Tyrone Fogle who have shared his knowledge and experiences with me. My family, friends, teachers, doctors, even my enemies too.

To my mother the late Lilly Scott who saw something in me, that other could not see. You have given me a chance at life I dedicated everything in my life to you. My two sisters Monica and Christina and two Brothers Shakeith and David. Thank You all for being by my side in everything I wanted to do.

I want to thank all of my spiritual family Shannon, Donessa Odom, Ms. Evelyn Workmen, Angela Barnett, Pastor Kevin Williams, James, thanks for pouring the word of God into my life.

Last but not least to everyone in the world with a disability you are the reason I wrote this book thank you.

"You are not disabled, but enabled to all capabilities, to all things that try and stop you."

Author Terrell Scott

CONTENTS

CHAPTER 1

Palsy Is the Name They Gave Me

"When I was conceived."

Drugs are bad; I learned that as a fetus from the time I was conceived. Throughout the nine months of my Mother's pregnancy, I was on drugs. Shortly after my arrival on January 22, 1989, I was given a name that labeled me for the rest of my life. It was the name people would identify me as. A name that I believed paralyzed my faith, knowledge, motivation and willingness to live the normal type life, I am Cerebral Palsy. Living with Cerebral Palsy was easier to adapt to when I was young because no one always reminded me of my disability when I was a child. As a child you do not think of anything other than being a kid, so having Cerebral Palsy meant nothing to me. I had to visit a therapist to gain strength in my body. My legs were bent in, and walking was tough for me. I had to wear a brace; my mother used to make me walk up and down the stairs. I did not understand it then but wearing the brace and the visits to the therapist help me walk better. Dealing with Cerebral Palsy did not make me feel any different than any of the other children. I played in the park with the other kids and even went to birthday parties. I had a few friends but not many, I saw myself as an average kid. However, I knew that something was indeed different about me. I had a rough start in life, but I have a great finish.

Your life has a Purpose

Who are we to question our lives when it was freely given to us from God? We just have to trust in Him. Have you ever thought of the reason for your life, the reason why you are here on earth? God have given us all a purpose, and He knew all about us before we were conceived in our mother's womb. He gave us the ability to get through every situation we face in our lives. When we are born, we are born innocent until the world exposes us to sin. Sin has influenced the minds of the people in this world. The enemy job is to kill, steal, and destroy. As we grow and mature we later find out that life have many obstacles, and after hitting rock bottom life teaches us that there is a pathway while trying to climb back up to the top. God put us through these things to test our faith. Sometimes God will give us things to show us we are not ready for the things we asked of Him. You were designed for this time and season; God has you here on earth for a reason. Truthfully, there is something He needs you to do that no one else can do. It is your time to plant the seed and to now reap the harvest. You have a gift that was hidden on the inside of you, that only God has given you. Just know that God can use anybody, no matter who you are, and just because you have a disability that doesn't mean God cannot use you. God still has a use for you. The life that you are living is someone else's deliverance. God loves you regardless of who you are, and regardless of what you have done. He does not look down on you, and He is not disappointed in you.

God's purpose for your life

Truthfully, we spend too much time doing everything in our lives that we simply ignore God. God's mission requires going through every test and passing everything He places before you. He will allow you to share your story with other people, to be someone else's blessing. He will change you, both inside and out. His will is for you to be successful. His will is for you to be great. His will is for you to prosper. You are designed to live through everything God has placed on the inside of you. Do not die without fulfilling your purpose, because your purpose dies with you. Your purpose is not passed on to the next person. God's purpose for you is not only for here on earth, but His purpose is for what He has for you in Heaven as well. When your time has come for you to leave this world, it means God has completed your purpose. Your purpose is helping other people, some of which you may you have not met yet get to their purpose in life. God has angels in Heaven to direct and guide you to get to what He has designed your purpose to be. God has a plan for your life. He designed you with a purpose and had given you vision on how you should live your life. When God gives you a vision, He shows you through a dream, and He tells you through prayer.

Your life has Visions

God gives us visions to show us what is to come in the future. Vision is a divine experience to manifest the reality of our lives. God talks to us through visions; He desires to change the outcome of the way we live our lives. Sometimes visions are not always clear to us. Satan then tries to come and interrupt what God has shown us in the vision. Satan distracts you from seeing what God has designed for you to do. Vision motivates the purpose for your life. God's people needs an image to motivate the vision. Without vision, the purpose for your life is not visible. God uses visions to communicate with us through the Spirit. Prophets use vision as a part of growth. People don't see us for who we are, but whom we can become. We all have imaginations, dreams, and goals that we want to accomplish in our lives. Vision structure, and panel out those dreams and goals to unfold what we see in our minds. If we apply the way that we think, to the way we envision our lives, then we can fulfill our purpose in God. You must have faith to do what God is showing you in the vision because without faith the vision is dead. Vision helps us to rely on God, and communicate with Him even more. God gives us visions to better understand who we are in Him. Visions provoke greatness, success, and promotions. God allows us to see things but doesn't always show us everything in the vision. We as people will try to predict how God is going to do something when he is not doing it in the way we thought he would. Sometimes God has an entirely different way because His thoughts are not like our thoughts.

You have wisdom

God gives each of us wisdom so that we will not perish. A lot of us perish, because of the lack of knowledge for our lives. We can all fulfill our purpose in God, but we first must have faith to What God is showing us in the vision. Without faith your vision is dead. The vision God has for you is not for everyone to see because people will use it as his or her own, and try to steal the blessings God has for you. When God created man, He planned and structured how He wanted your life to be. We often get discouraged, because our lives are not going the way we hope it will go. He does not want you to give up on yourself.

Seek God for your purpose and vision

Your downfalls are the breakthrough for your deliverance. You went through the storm, but now you can wait and see how God will bring you out. Ask him, what is the purpose for your life? Sometimes you may need understanding to what that purpose is, and God will give you a vision. There was a vision for your life even before you were conceived in your mother's womb.

Living with your disability

You as a disabled young adult are going to face many challenges as you go through life's journey. You will have some hard battles that will require much work. People will see the disability first before; they see your capabilities. Truthfully, everyone will not accept who you are. The biggest mistake is not a failure, but it is not trying after you failed.

Parents do not paralyze your child (ren) from doing the things they dream of doing.

I was rebellious to the things my family, friends, and doctors said that I was not capable of doing. There was a willpower in me said, that "I can." I have accomplished everything people thought that I would not be able to do. I know who I am, and I'm not Cerebral Palsy.

People will judge you on your appearances because most of them do not look at your heart.

"School."

How I felt about school, my teachers, and the other students is different from how I feel now.

Being in special Education happens for two reasons. For one, the child needs a little more help on learning school work materials, and the other, a child's behavior. It is not always because the child has a learning disability. You must have that mindset of "I can do this "I will make it." Do not let anybody tell you otherwise, or make you feel as though you cannot.

We are all different, but we can become equal if we all come together as one. Teachers limited their students on what they can and can't do. Instead of encouraging them on how they can succeed, and get their education. A lot of Special Education teachers downgrade their students. You the student have to encourage yourself, and push yourself to what you want to be done. Truthfully, some of the teachers will be no help in that area. Speak victory over your life, make it known to your teachers and others around you that, "My future is more successful than your limitation on my education."

Make education your top priority. Don't let criticism lower your self-esteem. How can a person learn something if they were never taught? Some students learning capabilities are on different levels, but it does not mean they are not capable of learning. Teachers have to follow what is on the student's IEP. Schools must decide to place a child with a disability if the child meets the requirements of special Education. When I was in school students who were in Special Ed learned the work according to what was on their IEP. Now special education students have the opportunity to graduate with a high school diploma even if they have an IEP. Parents you need to be more involved with your children's teacher. It is important that you go to the PTA (Parents Teachers Association) meetings. Parents you can help your child by being more involved with them while they are in school.

If your child is complaining about what is going on in the classroom, please listen to them. Do not always go by what the teachers are saying. Your children are our future. You are their stepping stone to help them succeed" I was a special education student, and going to school every day was hard because I was not learning what I needed for me to be successful. I was very determined to get my high school diploma. I was not going to let anybody or anything stand in my way. I was capable of learning everything that everyone else was learning. It was not just about an education, but I was setting the foundation for my life ahead.

Confidently working on a higher education

It was not until my 11th-grade year in high school that I was taking the classes that I needed to get my High School diploma. I received my high school certificate that stated I completed high school on graduation day, but I did not accept it. My teachers did not give me a chance to voice my opinion on anything, and if I tried to, they would not even listen to me at all. My teachers thought they knew what I could and could not do. Teaches your job is to educate, and not to discriminate. I believed in myself, and I fought hard to get to where I needed to be. My confidence in myself was stronger than anything my teachers tried to speak against me. I immediately applied for Adult education classes where I was able to transfer the credits I did receive from the high school.

Adult Ed was not that bad at all. I was getting the work I needed to graduate with a high school diploma. I was unable to complete Adult Ed because my family and I moved where I didn't have transportation. I had to stop going to school until August 2010. Due to my circumstances, I applied for Job Corps so that I could obtain my high school diploma. Job Corps required every student to be interviewed before being accepted into the program. Students must meet with an Admission

Counselor, and you must bring a picture ID, Social Security card, birth certificate, shot records, a criminal background check, and a one-page essay with you to the interview. My family helped me with all of those things I needed at that time.

I prayed every day and night; I never felt happier I was going away to school. I had a chance to prove to my love one's, family, and friends that I was going to make it. A few weeks after the interview I got a letter saying I was denied for being in the program. I was hurt, and all I could do was cry out to God. I called the Admission Counselor to question the reason for the denial. He stated," He didn't think I was capable or was ready to be in Job Corps." I pleaded for him to give me a chance to prove myself. Once again I was being judged on my appearance, the way I looked in the eyes of people. Prayer does change things, because at the beginning of January in 2011, I got a call for a second interview with the staff of the Bamberg, SC Job Corps. The interview went well the staff loved my personality, and was ready to work with me.

My first day was Feb 7, 2011; I completed the program in 8 months with my high school diploma and the Office Administration trade. They didn't even think I was going to make it no further than high school with a certificate. I was so blessed to have finally made it to College? Immediately after completing Job Corps, I enrolled into Denmark Technical College on my mother's birthday. I was so excited to give my mother the gift of entering into college on her birthday. My heart was filled with joy because the dream of getting a higher education finally came to pass. I enjoyed all my classes and all my teachers. Some of the students were very nice, while others still had the mindset of a high school student. I didn't enjoy living on campus it reminded me of my experiences in South Bronx, NY the projects. I completed my first semester with good grades, but I got expelled my second semester of my freshman year. I was being bullied and picked on with no help from the staff. I had every right to protect myself, or else my mother would have buried me. I politely went to the flea market and bought a pocket knife and a Taser. It's better to be alive and well than dead.

My love and passion for people allowed me to move to Hamlet, NC with some friends. It wasn't until our departure that I moved to

High Point, NC. Living out on my own started out good, but it also was a major struggle for me. I maintain all my bills on a fixed income. I would explain that later in another book.

Living Without Limitations

My heart desire was always to reach out to disabled adults. I want to reach out to young men and women with a disability to motivate them to stand out and don't be afraid to succeed in life. I want to help them to dodge the bullet of failure, depression, disappointment, sorrow, loneliness, sickness, and manipulation. Live your life, and let God be your Guide. The most painful thing is losing you in the process of trying to better yourself, even while others try pushing you down. People don't notice you until you are successful, but when you are least to make it you become their last choice. Don't let anyone look down on you or make you feel like you can't, because you can. What you speak out your mouth manifests into the atmosphere. This means if you believe it can happen all you have to do is believe it can. You were born with a disability, but you are not disabled to live your life. The disabled one is the gifted one. You are disabled, but God is able. Please don't limit yourself to the things you can and cannot do. Truthfully, with God, there are no limits. In Philippians 4:13, it states,

"You can do all things through Christ, Who strengthens you."

Every day you wake up to ask God to strengthen you. You have the ability to do whatever you want to do with your life. You weren't created by God to struggle and die. You are what you accept; then you become the very thing that you believe you are. The potentials are there indeed, but people can't see it because they can't get through your image. If we didn't have different characters, our identity and reflection would be the same. We all are human so why can't we live our life the same. We can't live life the same because we are all gifted with different talents. If nobody didn't tell you this today, "You are anointed by God." God gifts everyone, but don't have the anointing of

God. You were born with a disability, but some people were born with all type of things such as sicknesses, or even illnesses. Some may have missing arms or even missing legs. We are not made to see gender, race, disabilities, religion, or even sexualities. Fight for what you want in life. Do not take "no" for an answer.

You have to make people believe that you can do the same things that they can do. People don't think much of a disabled person, and they don't try to. We have all different types of individuals in the world, different personalities, hearts, and spirits. Some people are friendly, and some people are mean. Some people are just selfish to their self-pity. People will judge you before they get to know you. The sad thing is that we all have a past, and we all came from something bad, so there is no room to judge. Sadly, people still judge you. Don't ever think you're not good enough. If a person can't see how amazing you are, then they don't need to be in your life. If people are absent during your struggles, then they don't need to be present during the success in your life. Don't hate on my respect or my confidence that I have for myself. Just hate the fact that you need to be more like me. Even when you are under so much pressure, but God got you still standing. You are not going to break down easily because there is a purpose for you. You shall overcome any, and every obstacle that you face. Believe me, that better day is on the way for you, and when they come it's going to be blissful. You deserve it! When I look back and see where I came from, a lot of times I cry tears of appreciation. I cry because I thank God that I'm not a product of my past. Struggles are stepping stones so we can use them to rise to the top, or they'll fall, and you'll sink to the bottom.

Living Out A Dream

I am 26 years old, and there is so much more life ahead of me. I may be young, but I have had my fair share of obstacles to get through. Through it all, I have come out on top, and stronger than I was before. My dreams and goals are right in front of me. They are calling for me to achieve them. They sound loud, but I am getting closer to them every single day. Some say that striving for your dreams may be foolish, but it's not what others say it's what you feel in your heart.

I can't wait for the day I can tell my family to quit their job so that I can take care of them. Let them live the life they deserve to live. I can't wait for that day where all of my dreams becomes a reality. For that day where I look up in Times, and space knowing that there was a supernatural change in my life. I can't wait for the day where every disabled person has a smile on their faces not feeling down for anything in their lives. I can't wait for that very day where I look into the eyes of every disabled person, and they say my life is better now I feel like a normal person for the first time in my life.

Realizing that the vision I had made a significant impact for us all. Of course, they have identified us as being retarded. This day is a dream that will become my reality of all disable people to live the way our God wants it to be. I can't wait for that day where our happiness, peace, and joy strengthen us to where we no longer feel disabled again. God has his ways and reasons for allowing certain events to happen in your lives at certain times. I trust in Him.

Success, prosperity, health, and wealth. It will all come one day, and I shall wait. Continue to live my life the way I know God planned it to be. I will do just what GOD said to do. We live, and we learn. Take a step forward in your life and put your priorities in order, and don't worry about the next person in line. It is odd how we all pass judgment; normally it's a negative comment. Don't pass a judgment you wouldn't want pass on to you.

Disabled people can't talk, walk or move, but they still can feel and hear the things that are said against them.

communication is key

Disabled people communicate with sound and movement or their bodies. You may not be able to understand, but that doesn't mean there is no communication, because if you just listen you hear them. As we live our lives, we find ourselves in situations that needs much attention. The immediate reaction is what we may need. We as people of the world have gotten to the point where we don't want God, or feel we don't need Him. What God has to do is He have to step back while silently watching over us. He shows us that we are nothing without Him.

Those who are faithfully walking with God he is just testing your faith in Him in the situation. The teacher is always quiet during the test. The best way to build a relationship with God is giving your life completely over to Him. Making a covenant with God, you are making an agreement with God. Have you ever written a contract with someone for something, such as a cell phone? You made a deal for two years. Your contract with God is the same way, but He protects you forever.

He will guide you into your purpose. We as a disabled adult cannot trust people with our feelings. People will use and abuse you if you let them. People feel that they can get away with the wrong they do if they are not caught doing so. The covenant between you and God will protect you just like insurance protects individuals who are in accidents. You must also watch out for the ones who proclaim to be your friends. They are out to get your money, but not your friendship. Some people mishandle the disabled. They are beating and hitting on them. Using file language against them. If you can speak up tell someone that you trust. If not use body language, and point your finger at the abuser. How can you hurt something that is defenseless to hurt you? Can you feel the pain that you are causing to somebody else? You can physically damage someone from the inside because it isn't showing from the outside that doesn't mean it's not there treat those how you treat yourself. Love comes from, emotion feelings thoughts and action. Love can be harmful or good base on the heart you have. Disabled people have feelings too so don't treat them like an object. When you look in the mirror what do you see? How do you view yourself as a person? Do you see yourself as a person? Do you think of yourself as a cripple person who can't do anything with yourself?

We all come in different shapes, sizes, big, small, short, and tall. Our character and personality tell people who we are. You are whom you say you are. So become whom you believe that you are.

CHAPTER 2

I Can Do It, And I Will Make

Surviving in spite of challenges

Trying to survive out here on my own was difficult for me because people made it difficult for me. Living in a world where society is careless about other people's feelings, I was always told I couldn't do this or that, because of my disability. I felt miserable, and the world I was living in felt useless, but the only thing I had was my faith in God. I had a relationship with Him, and I knew He had a purpose for my life.

You can't let people control your life; because your thoughts, emotions, and feelings don't belong to their hearts. It is your heart unless you make a choice to let them into it.

Your heart was giving to you by God.

We all have a talent that can help us succeed in life. Maybe you can dance, sing, draw, design, cook or write music, books. Your talent was given to you for you to be successful in life. If you think big, you will receive big. If you think small, you will receive small, if your thoughts are unlimited anything can happen. It's not that people can't, people are not trying to. Don't settle for what you are used to.

Communication with God

What is a mind without thoughts? What's love without the heart? You have to live your life the way you want to not the way people tell you. The mind of a disabled person is stronger than anyone else's because it's not publicized for the world to invade. You may be other people's last choice, but you were God's first pick. There is nothing in this world that happens without God not being in it.

The best way to communicate with God is through praying and fasting. When you fast, you turn down your plate, and sacrifice your food. God will only reveal things to you about your life when you turn everything else away to seek Him and the directions for your life. During your fasting periods, the nights seem much easier than days. The hardest day is the third day because your body will start to react without food. The last two days will be a breeze for you, because your heart, mind, and soul are meditating on the will of God. Once you have made a vow to God, you will be tested. Things that you do in your life that are not of God will come against you again and again. How do you pass your test? You must stay in the will of God; read the word of God, quote the word of God, and live it daily. The best way is to seek God by praying to Him to guide your life during the hardest times. We were not put on Earth for ourselves, but for other people. We fail every time we think of ourselves and are not considerate of other people. They may not accept you the first three times, but eventually, they will learn to accept you for who you are, put away their flaws and preferences and love you for you.

Sometimes you are better alone than having people in your corner. The fewer people in your life, the less you have to worry about getting hurt. You can always tell how a person love you by their actions or the words they use because true love will always reveal itself through a person's heart/ The world doesn't know anything about you. They only know what they see on the outside of you. We the desirable, inspirational, sufficient, affectionate, blessed, loved exceptional ones. God appoints us all the (disabled) one.

Living under the laws

America has been living under the legislation of the government and forgot who wrote these laws. The government has corrupted the minds of people who are disabled and are receiving benefits from social security. The government wants you to believe you are not able to do anything while in the system. Disabled people have the ability to live their lives and accomplish their goals as well. Disabled people are not useless or powerless.

Disabled people must strengthen their minds and physical bodies. Do not use your benefits as a clutch. The government can shut down and can threaten to stop your benefits at any given time. It's important for you to go out and do something with yourself. If the government stops giving you benefits, and you have no education or any job experience, you will be left without.

It's a hurtful feeling to be without or denied for something that you want to do. If everyone denies you, then you will begin to deny yourself. The government and society made you believe you are nothing. Not being active can cause you to be depressed.

Struggling and the economy

The economy right now doesn't pay enough money. People are struggling and going without. Poverty is in familiar places of the world. Americans are living freely, but are nothing without government assistance. Americans are living on the streets and are going hungry because they have no income at all. Disabled people must be taught how to manage money, and learn how to live out on his or her own. Disabled people can volunteer at different places to gain job experience. I encourage the disabled young adult to stand out, take chances, to avoid poverty and homelessness. I knew at an early age in life that I needed an education, and a job to be able to succeed in life. I worked hard to be successful, but I didn't have any support from anyone. Sometimes you have to help yourself when you do not have someone else to support you. You are your greatest support. People will not support what is not beneficial to them. The lack of support is the biggest issue in America. We are one, and everything works together with the support from one another. We spend too much time looking down on one another that we fail ourselves. People will let you fall and then walk right over you before they help pick you up. Everybody isn't for you. Most people believe they are better than you because you have a disability. Disabled people have a lack of support because there are individuals who feel that you are abusing the system. Everyone does not abuse the system. The money that is given is not even enough to maintain a well-balanced life. The money is enough just to get you through a month or two. The government needs to put out more organizations, and programs for the disable people to get into while they are receiving benefits. The programs should allow disabled young adults to maintain a job earning extra money that will be put precisely into a savings account. The savings account will allow the disable to manage bills, and help with their personal needs. How do the government expect you to live off a fixed income that is received once a month, and not struggle at the end of the month? We have to live just like everyone else is living. Living on a fixed income or no income at all is stressful, and it's sorrowful. Disabled people are not animals, and we do not live in cages. So, therefore, stop treating us as such. Disabled people feels worthless at times, and want to do so much more. They watch their fellow peers accomplish many goals, only wishing it could be them. The government put us in scary situations. Causes us to question ourselves, and to ask questions. Questions like, what will happen if? Can I do this? We are fearful of losing the income if we go out and work, and once we start working will we be able to maintain the job and keep it? I'm tired of being scared. What is a risk if we don't go out and take it? The change starts with you, just go out there and take the risk. Silent the noise of the world, and paralyze everything they try to use against you to keep you from moving forward. Use other people's failures to motivate you to achieve the things that you always wanted to accomplish in your life.

CHAPTER 3

Be Wise, You Are Not Alone

Wisdom gives us the ability to have knowledge. With this knowledge, we could have the understanding to be able to identify our circumstances and enable us to get through every situation that we may face. God gave us the wisdom of interpretation, the wisdom of interpretation helps recognize the things that are of God, and the things that are not of God.

We must be wise to know the spirit and the truth of God. God gave everyone some wisdom to be able to live in this world. He gave you the wisdom to live a life of the natural, and life of the spiritual if you are born again. Man can influence people who live a life of the natural deal with things of the world, and. Everything that connected to the kingdom of God is the spiritual life. We have access to the kingdom of God through fasting and praying, living by the commands and the laws of God, this gives us full access to Jesus. Wisdom is the key to knowing right from wrong. The knowledge of being wise will allow you to choose the way you want to live.

Being kept by God

I felt like a dead man walking, but my faith in God kept my hope alive. A few years ago before I became as successful as I am today, I had nobody but myself. I was always sad but didn't shed any tears, never showed any signs of weakness or depression. People already didn't see much good in me.

This joy that I have

Showing my weakness gave others permission to kill what little bit of joy that I had on the inside of me. The pain that I felt no one could have taking that away, no one but the Lord Jesus Christ. I didn't want to eat, nor bathe myself. I wasn't interacting with anybody because everyone who was a part of my life made me feel they were more successful than me. I was slowly fading away from the world while living in the world. You can't allow people in this world to get you to a point where you don't want to live. Even when I spent the time with myself, I knew I wasn't alone, because God was always with me. I prayed for everything in my life. God was all that I had.

I wish God were in the physical, but He's more powerful in the supernatural. The life we live was not a choice that we made; neither was it a decision our parents made. God planned the life we live; we just have to trust and believe in Him. God's will is not our will. We all have a heart desire that we want to fulfill, but God's will be far greater than the desires of our heart. Seek the full knowledge of God so that you will understand the real power of His glory. Everyone in this world will face happiness, sadness, peace and joy. Our lives weren't created to be a joyful experience because Heaven would have already been our home. We're all going to go through things God put us through; this will determine whom we are truly living for?

Course of life

We all have bear the fruit we eat from.

Lives are about opportunities, chances, and consequences. You live and learn that life has its course. The course you decide to take will determine what you will go through in your life. When you do well, you are honored with awards of recognition. When you do things that are bad, you are sentenced to punishment. We all have things we have to deal with in our lives no matter what race, religion, sexuality, or even your disabilities. We all are bearing the fruit that we ate. People are sick, homeless, poor, and disabled. There is something wrong with every one of us. Trouble and consequences don't see age or race and it don't discriminate against the life it wants to repay.

We are one but unequally divided

As an African American, I know that we are sometimes seen as if we are the only race that comes against one another. We are thought to be jealous of one another because one has something the other don't have, but that is not true. Why do we have to look a certain way in order be accepted by someone else? Sadness, pain, and sorrow are very well hidden then it is shown. People don't show those feelings, but they try to handle it on their own. Keeping those emotions bundled up will eat at you from the inside. Those feelings are eating at your heart. The heart can't handle extreme sadness, pain, and sorrow. Your heart will begin to tell your mind to kill the body. God is a God of goodness. Those bad emotions are not of God; they are of the devil. People are all worn out and have reached their limit, and have taken all they can take. Reaching out to the world that seems to be so loud, but people are silent when it has nothing to do with them. The person feels so alone because no one notices the pain that he or she are in until he or she are found dead. Suicide is not the answer to ending your problems. If your soul isn't right your problems, die with you and live with you in Hell. The world has lost so many talented people that the world has destroyed. How can you throw dirt on top of dirt then call the dirt clean? There isn't anyone on planet earth that is perfect. You can't sit high and look low on me because my mess is not about your mess. People cover up the things they don't want to be penalized for. Some things in life can seem to be unreal because it's not visible to the worldview of today. You may not see every circumstance; you may never understand every problem; a solution may never be an answer but just embracing the fact that a person isn't the only person going through a situation may be the cure to the problem. Without wisdom, you can become naive to the things of the world, and ignorant to the will of God. If you don't have knowledge of what God will is for your life, then you can become disobedience to the will of God.

CHAPTER 4

The Divine Revelation of my life

Cerebral Palsy has played a big part in my life. It held onto me like a clutch, as if it was providing for my life. People will mark you before reading your story. You can't judge everyone by their appearance, because if you look on the inside, you will see something far much greater than what's on the outside. You never know the prize that is waiting on the inside until you look inside of the box. In my early teenage years on to adulthood, I became isolated from everything that dealt with fun activities because I felt like I couldn't keep up with the other kids or adults. I knew my muscle and bones wasn't strong as the other kids, so I didn't engage in any of the activities willingly. At times I was pushed into participating myself. Growing up to accept whom I am taking the love of God, because everything about me God already knew. He had a plan for me; He has one for you too. I was born on January 22, 1989, in Bronx, New York. I was raised by my mother who adopted me a few months after I was born. I have three siblings; I have two sisters and one brother. We later moved to South Carolina where we all attended and graduated from High School, while my brother stayed behind in New York. My mother loved all her children and had a love for other children as well. She was a mother first at all times, a good friend to many, and a loving Teacher to many of her students.

Appreciating my life challenges

My mother later died on November 20, 2013, where she left behind four children and family.

She carried a lot on her shoulders which stressed my mom out. I wasn't too much of a bad kid, but I was always misunderstood, I misbehaved in school. I was very disrespectful to my mom. I didn't mean to be just wanted to be heard while trying to accept who I was. My mother was in a very abusive relationship that affected my siblings and I. He was the type that took discipline way too far. I disliked him for it, but I appreciate it now. I am much wiser, I'm much better, and I am much stronger. Those beatings turned me into the young man of God that I am today.

I don't agree with abuse, and I'm not saying he was right but, I'm not on the streets dead or locked up.

My view on Mental Health

My mother did what any loving Mother would do for their child; she got me some help. She took me to mental health, and before the behavior problems started, I was already labeled. The doctors could never determine what the problem was so they just medicated me. I didn't like going to mental health, because going there made me felt like I was a handicap. Mental health can help with psychological problems, but personally, I think it can stop young people from progressing. Every issue doesn't need to be medicated. Mental health is setting us up for failure and blocking our capabilities of being successful in life.

Dealing with life challenges

We as young black men are being looked at as criminals. We are targeted by policemen who wants us off the streets. The fear they have is not a war or riot. They fear black men becoming businessmen with degrees.

The best way to help a person with disabilities is to listen and learn what their capabilities are before placing a label on them. Everybody is capable of doing something if you learn a person's abilities. I decided I no longer wanted help from mental health. I wanted to go out and learn the world for myself. I believed if we had the right people in our corners, and having a good support system in life; we will be able to accomplish many things.

My problem was feeling left out, feeling as if nobody cared for me, or loved me. I didn't have any friends at school, but the ones I did associate with made me felt left out. I guess my appearance made people not want to talk to me. I suppose they felt their group of friends would judge them if they were seen talking to me. The sad thing of it all is they missed out on the blessings that were connected to me.

Somebody now, somewhere who knew me in my past are reading my book. I know they are in total shock right now. All I can say was when I needed a friend; you didn't care to be my friend. If you weren't there when I tried to be a friend to you, then I know you are shocked on how God is using me now. God has tremendously blessed me. I'm not going to do what you did to me. I will treat you by greeting you with a smile, giving you encouraging words, and desire you to continue to be who you are. Don't miss out on another blessing through the person you didn't admire too much.

Walking In Love without being love

When you have been let down so many times as I have, you learn not to count on other people to respect your feelings? I expected everyone to mishandle me, but everyone isn't the same. Respect people even if they do not respect you. Every good deed that you do may not look at, but God sees it. Every good thing you do is recorded in Heaven. Love can only have to mean if the attention of it has value to the heart. The way to find out if a person is sincere about love is to question it. You need to know why they are in love with you. People can love you for all the wrong reasons. Recognize the attention they give you. I finally realized people wasn't going to love me in the way I care and love them because everyone wasn't going to accept me. What isn't seen can easily be misunderstood, especially if it is not explained. I continued to show love to people, but being rejected push me closer to God, but I still wanted to be with someone.

I have been fighting homosexuality for over nine years. I knew being one isn't the will of God, so I fought it every day of my life. I never admitted and owned up to being gay, because I knew what the word said. People often says," God loves you no matter what, "yes He does, but He does not love the sin. One thing I hate with a passion, and that is being rejected. I hate not being wanted, because nobody is perfect. For we all are human, and we all should be trying to get into Heaven.

The women in my family are known for having a good heart and having a love for Children. I know I would have been a great dad and a great husband to my wife. Females rejected me so much until it pushed me into the arms of a man. The love of a man in this lifestyle is deceiving and tricky. You cannot trust the word "love" without the actions of the word. Sadness, pain, and sorrow will reveal true love, because being hurt will tell if a person loves you.

Our ways are not always like God

I only met guys over the internet, because I did not have the approval of my family. Truthfully, I never hid it from them. The internet is dangerous and has all kinds of people using it. I kept people I talked to away, and I regretted this homosexual lifestyle. It became evident that the people only wanted me for sex or money. Being young and naive I thought a few kind words and sex meant love.

My second encounter was with a man whom I saw at a party; I was invited too. When I first saw this guy I knew I was not going to talk to him, because he was not my type. I was in my feelings that no one cared enough to talk to me at the party. On May 10, 2008, I saw this guy again at the library, and he passed me a note asking me "Do you want to have sex today?" I replied yes. We both logout our computers we got in his car, and he took me to a spot, and we had sex. I had no idea from that day on this guy change my life forever because he gave me HIV. I still to this day haven't cried about it, I just had to accept it.

Everything happens for a reason, but throughout this journey, I have stayed strong in the Lord.

My first thought was "I will not die of this disease." Don't allow the disease to have you, but have control over the disease. Please don't pass judgment over me, because you do not know what I had to go through before I took control over HIV. No one knows how, where, or even when he or she will die. We all know that one day that we will die. Don't assume because a person is sick they will die because they can be in any situation that God allows to happen to take their life. Well, I only met one other guy whom I met on a Video Chatting site, which I am no longer friends with who accepted me for my HIV. He lived in North Carolina, whom I knew over six months and moved in with. The kind of friendship we had was the things couples would only do. We shared feelings while doing nice things for one another, but our relationship ended after we moved to our new apartment in High Point, North Carolina.

A total surrender

This is where my journey continued. I found a church that I now attend and became a member. I wanted to fully give my life to Christ after years of being saved. I decided to get baptized by my Pastor at our church on September 6, 2014. Once being baptized that does not mean every bad thing will go away because that is when it gets harder. Being baptized is so God can test you and to see who are you living for You are either living for Him or you are living of the world. Earth is not my home. To God, I belong.

My weary days will only come when I do not trust in Him, but my good days will forever be the best days of my life when I trust in Him. I may not look like my best days, but never will my worst days be a part of my appearance. I know that God is the cure for the very thing that man said wouldn't be any cure. By His stripes, I am already healed.

Author Terrell Scott

CHAPTER 5

Obedience Will Get You Through

Free will gives you the ability to live your life willingly, without being prosecuted for the way you choose to live your life. You can believe in whatever religion you want to believe in without being judged or even killed. Demonstrating free will won't give room for others to judge you for who you are as a person. Free will allows you to choose the character that you display before others. Free will also open avenues for you to make choices of your very own. With free will, you can express who you are as a person. You can express your sexuality, personal beliefs, religion, and not be judged by God. People may judge you, but God won't. God loves you, and that's why He gave you free will. God will never force you into loving Him. This is why free will allows you to choose whom you will live with.

God gave us laws to live by, and these laws are known as The Ten Commandments.

The Laws of God
(Exodus 20:1-17)

We have to live by these commandments and be obedient to all ten of them. It's better to obey and submit to the will of God then to be prosecuted by God. Obedience will give you opportunities of natural growth throughout your life. Don't be penalized for not being obedient. Obedience will help you conduct yourself in the right way while living in this world. We often ignore rules by doing things our way and not what the rules tell us to do. Disobedience is nothing more than trails and tribulation that will take years to come out of. Your way isn't always the right way. Disobedience is always the wrong way, but doing as you are told will always keep you going in the right way. Why must we learn the hard way by not doing as we are told to get it right? Trouble don't last always, but disobedience will never give you an easy way out.

Understanding the importance of obedient

We often think that rules and regulations are always too strict. Rules were put in place to keep everything in order, so when danger or anything that is outside of the rules happens there will be a safe way out. You may not understand it now, but without rules, life will teach you why it's so important to have them. Please be obedient, because obedience helps prepares you on different things that lie ahead. You want people to be able to trust you, not disregard you because of the choices you made.

The reason why I'm living with HIV is that I wanted to listen to everybody else instead of listening to my mother. I thought she was too strict, but I didn't realize she was protecting me from the very thing she was afraid that would happen to me. I felt like I could do anything on my own. I had to realize that my Mother's love for me was stronger than my will, and the selfishness of my very heart.

Don't allow people to influence you to do what isn't the right thing for you to do. If the choices you've made has not caught up with you already, then just keep on living. Sometimes it will happen when you least expect it to. Being obedient will save you from being hurt, sharing tears, and problems. Obedience will lead you to great things in your life. God will never leave nor forsake you; His desire is for you to be with Him. Just trust that His ways will never be our ways, but trusting in Him is the way of God. Obedience will make you lose some things and gain somethings, but don't be afraid of giving up the things you love. Your obedience to God's will can give you more than what you have right now. Obedience is always better than sacrifice because disobedience there will be no sacrifice.

You will lose more than you will gain because losing will keep you from letting go the very things that you love. If letting go of the materialistic things in your life is hard, then it was never beneficial to you from the start. A lot of worldly things is keeping you from doing the will of God. What isn't the will of God will surely go against the will of God for your life. How many times do you have to fail before you can get it right? Continually making the same mistakes over and over again is no longer a mistake, it's a personal choice. Some people don't want to live their life right. The only time they want to do right is when the choices they have made come back and attack their lives. Attack them until they no longer can carry out the bad choices they have made in the past, and only God can bring them out.

It's funny how God isn't necessary until we face problems in our lives. This is the only time some of us acknowledge God. You need to praise God in every situation that you in because we all need Him. Call on Him during your times of trouble, Call on God during of your Joyful days. Call on God in the midst of your tears, Call on God when you are praising and worshipping Him. We should never cease calling on God. You want God to receive your worship does not reject it.

Let's look at the word of God for more references. The Bible declares:

"Not every one that saith unto me, Lord, Lord, shall enter into the kingdom of heaven; but he that doeth the will of my Father which is in heaven."

Matthew 7:21

You do not want to be turned away when you need God the most. The reason why most people will be turned away is that they do not acknowledge God, so God will not recognize them.

"Obedience to God"

Keep My Commandments

"If you love me you will keep my commandments "(John 14:15)

Living by his commandments show loyalty to God by your heart and not by mouth. We can say we love something and don't act upon what we say. God know you by what's in your heart.

It's Through Your obedience

"If you are willing and obedience, you shall eat the good of the land. "(Isaiah 1:19)

Obedience to God is substance to all things good, and you will not lack, need or want for nothing. Everything you need GOD's got it through your obedience.

The define word for substance.

Substance (noun)

The subject matter of thought, discourse, study, etc.

Be Obedient in Everything You Do

"For this is why I wrote that I might test you and know whether you are obedience in everything" (2 Corinthians 2:9)

Be obedience in everything that you do so that your obedience is recognized by your heart.

Those who are members of the body of Christ will go through the storm, but obedience will cast the wind and the rains of the storm away.

A dark heart is a wicked one it hides in the shadow of evil. Everyone does not have the heart of God. The wicked one will do evil and live their lives as evil ones and won't be brothers. The righteous one of a kind heart will do wicked and have the conviction of God.

Make It Count

Thinketh in his heart so is he: Eat and drink, saith he to thee; but his heart is not with thee.

God allow. (Proverbs 23:7)

Live your life in the way you want to, be mindful that everything you do you will be accounted for. Everything you do is being recorded. You can't cheat or mishandle God because He already knew all the things you would do in life because He Is God!

Be not deceived; God is not mocked: for whatsoever a man soweth, that shall he also reap. Galatians (6:7)

CHAPTER 6

Living Your Life With Confidence

Faith Helps You Be More Productive In Life

Stop allowing what other people say control how you live your life. Be Confident in the person God made you. Nobody can live your life but you and you alone. You came into this world alone, and you will die alone. Everything you have will not follow you to the grave, but the impact of your life will remain here. Your impact will touch the lives of people who are going through tough situations in their lives. How many times have other people decisions caused you to miss out on opportunities that God wanted you to have? Don't listen to people who don't even have a perpendicular direction to the path of their life, to even try to lead you through yours. Opportunities are often missed out on, because we go with what other people lead us to, instead of going in the direction that our faith leads us. Discrimination which is the lack of motivation criticism is what stopping you from pursuing greatness in your life. What are you afraid of? You don't know if you are fearful without going out experiencing things and testing the waters. You are not scared if you don't go out into the world and experience things out. What is your motive? Do you have the motivation to succeed in life? Have you reached all of your dreams? Did you set out your goals for your future? We as the black community are living what our leaders try to prevent from happening. We have the lack of fear, and we are not afraid that history is repeating itself. God is in control of every situation, so let Him handle what you can't handle. Start living the life of what has already been changed, and stop living the life that was fought to be changed. You can live the changed life. Accept who you are, and embrace your true identity. Be truthful, and die with the conviction of knowing who you are. Once you have identified whom you are, and accepted your own truth, then who can come against you? No one can come to you, other than yourself. Live your life in confidence and believe that you can achieve anything that you want. There will be people who will try to stop you because they don't believe you can do anything. Just remember they are not the ones who are living the life that God has given you. We know whom we are, and have accepted that we were born with a disability. Living with a disability can be difficult, but we need to build confidence in ourselves. There will be people who will knock us down every time we try to accomplish a goal, and they will still refer to us as being retarded. I never agreed with the word "retarded." Retarded is assigned to a person without the sense or knowledge of what's going on. Confidence will help you get through those negative things that try to come against you. With confidence, you will be able to triumph over all obstacles that come your way. These barriers may come from many directions. You cannot make it without confidence. Just simply trying to live life without confidence is like living life without Jesus.

The Power of Conviction

Conviction makes you feel guilty to every sin and wrong doing. If we allow ourselves to yield to the Holy Spirit, then we live a better life. God allows us to be able to make choices. Conviction is a powerful thing. If you enable it to, it will stop you before you do the very wrong thing that is a sin. Conviction leads you into the right direction. Don't put your confidence into a man not even in yourself. You will get let down each and every time. Your confidence should always be in God.

When the will of God was removed from the country living a normal life wasn't possible anymore.

Wickedness is in the hearts of those in the midst of the falling angels. God's grace is upon us, and without His mercies, the nation has fallen. Confidence in yourself will push you to move forward in your life when you don't have the courage to do so.

Look at this, the late Dr. Maya Angelou wrote:

"Words mean more than what it set down on paper. It takes the human voice to infuse them with shades of deeper meaning. I've learned that people will forget what you said, people will forget what you did, but people will never forget how you made them feel. While the rest of the world has been improving technology, Ghana has been improving the quality of man's humanity to man."

Dr. Maya Angelou

Why worry about the things that won't last always. We just have to pray for the things that we have, and desire. We have to learn to focus on the good things in life, and not the bad. Those good things will make your life worth living. The negative things around you can only stay if you are holding on to them. I remember so many negative things that happened in my life. I remember the good, bad, and the ugly. I have been called so many names, but I only answer to one.

Tyler Perry quotes:

"It's not what people call you; it's what you answer too."

Tyler Perry

I am going to be what I believe I am. I accept what people are afraid to become and that's the disability I was born with. I strive for the best things in life. My wellbeing may not mean anything to you, but it means the world to me. Many want their names to be recognized by the world, but I only want my name to be written in the Lamb's book of life. I want to hear the angels rejoicing, and I want to throw my crown at the feet of Jesus. I have been called many different names that I know is not good for anyone's growth. Be happy about who you are. Don't be disappointed about your mishaps, and things that you can't change. I have confidence in you, and I believe that you can make it. That you are many things, but a failure you're not. I believe that you have the confidence needed to live your life with happiness, and no regrets.

God is the Creator

God's creation starts with life, and God's creation ends with death. Everything that you are is because of God, and everything that exist is because of God. There is nothing in this world that God hasn't done. You are whom God called you to be. If somebody has a problem with the way you look, walk, or talk, tell them to take it up with God. It's because God created everything, and everything that you and I are made of is because of Him. We are one nation under God and not one nation under man. Stop accepting what God have not created your life to be. You have power in your tongue, so start declaring and decreeing good things over your life. Tell the devil to get behind you. Stand on the head of the serpent, and let God fight your battles. Do not stress yourself out trying to get people to accept you, because you will kill yourself trying to get people to like you. There is only one who is perfect, and that is Jesus Christ.

"Live today, forget yesterday, and leave tomorrow up to God."

Author Terrell Scott

Our worldly rights

People hide disappointments very well and don't want others to see the pain there are going through. Live your life not only with confidence but with dignity. You have the right to live a happy, and peaceful life. You also have the right to freedom of speech. You have just as many rights to this world as anybody else. I was always told to treat others in a way you want to be treated. Many people don't live by that golden rule. People will treat you just the way they want, and it doesn't matter how nice you are to them. Continue to live by those golden rules no matter how angry you get.

What you say and do will always come back on you. Wrongfully mistreating others may not come when you do it, but it will show up in the times when you are not expecting it. You don't owe anyone anything just because you look, walk, and talk in a certain way. Yes, it may take you a while to come to the knowledge of what is happening around you, but that's why we should pray for wisdom in all things. People will criticize you, and they will also judge you.

If people stop judging others over their circumstances, then this will be a much better place to live. I never understood why people are such concern with the way other people live their lives. The ones that seem to be a concern are the people who are not doing anything to better themselves. Instead of putting people down, we need to start lifting people up. Let's do this without talking behind other's back, and do it out of genuine love. God is the Creator, and you are the creation. So live your life as a creation and not as a disabled person. Disability is not a part of your character, because the inside you don't feel like you are disabled. It's ok for a person never to like you for who you are. People may never talk to you or may look at you funny. Never accept being disrespected, not even from a preacher.

Words can make a person day even brighter, or it can cause your day to be sad. Words can also hurt a person from the inside, and break them down. The phrase,

"Sticks and Stones may break my bone, but words will never hurt" was a lie to cover up the damage that will follow you all the days of your life.

CHAPTER 7

Walk of Integrity

Having Integrity Is Important

Live your life with integrity, each and every step that you take. You should never be ashamed in your walk with God. Do not doubt, or be hypocritical. Live without any doubt. Know that you don't have to doubt God's love for you, and your love for Him. Understand that God has accepted you for who you are. Integrity is what Christians should practice, and live it every day. Have faith in your walk of integrity, and keep your eyes on things that are sweet as honey. Let integrity lead you when you stumble along the way. During your journey, you will stumble. Integrity will bless those who are sincere with their walk, but those who have a crook in their walk are not righteous.

Scripture records:

"He that walketh uprightly walketh securely: but he that perverts his ways shall be known." (Proverbs 10:9)

"The integrity of the upright shall guide them, But the perverseness of the transgressor shall destroy them."

(Proverbs 11:3)

Let thine eyes look right on, and let thine eyelids look straight before thee

(Proverbs 4:25)

Be True To Who You Are

Take pride in who you are with integrity, and never forget the truth of who you are while alive.

There will be people who will get in the way of your integrity, trying to discourage you. Remember always to be kind no matter what they say or do to you. People always come against those who are weaker than they are, because they think they are getting away with the things that they do.

Those who do wrongfully to others are never getting away with it; you are just getting by. You are blind with absolutely no knowledge of the wrong you are doing to others. This indeed is a trick of the devil. We as Christians should not return the favor with evil works because we will be just as wrong as you are. Christians should forgive you for what you've done. Every time we forgive you, God forgives us for our sins. Coming to the knowledge of the mistakes you made is a man with integrity. Spitefully wrongdoing, and knowingly in your heart with your head held up high makes you a coward.

Truthfulness should always be in your heart while walking with integrity. If you are not true to yourself, your walk of integrity is a lie. If you are untruthful in your walk, that makes every step you take hypocrisy. You never had confidence in the moral beliefs that you are somebody other than a person with a disability. You let others get inside your head, and there is shame in your walk of integrity. Integrity reveals your real character while you are under pressure. Integrity brings peace to your inner self. Ask yourself these three questions:

Do you mean what you say?

Are you doing what you say?

Is there any meaning to the words which you speak out of your mouth?

Speak integrity out of your mouth. Live the words that you speak with your whole heart. The words you speak have power in them. The word integrity from the Dictionary means:

"Adherence to moral and ethical principles; soundness of moral character; honesty."

Ethical means you know right from wrong. You should always remain the same dealing with your character and moral beliefs. Anything outside your character will always reveal itself.

"Wrong is not always right; sometimes personal truth has a white lie knowing the different between the two is integrity from the heart."

Always stay true to yourself. Who can love you better than you? Never step outside your character, because others have mishandled your integrity. People of the world thinks just because we are Christians and inside the Church, we won't retaliate to the negative things that come against us. We are not perfect, but we still make mistakes. There's no such thing as a Christian who lives right every day without making a mistake. We might not act out on what we want to do, but we often think it. It reminds us of whom we use to be before we got saved. Integrity should be like God giving grace even though we have sinned and didn't deserve it. The good things that are giving to us, but it's still handed to us only because of the favor of God. That how you should treat the people who mishandled you. Always have integrity in and out closed doors. You can't be a nice loving person with a good heart in one place, but not be a loving person in another. Who you are will reveal itself through your action, response, and your speech. God is in every situation there is nothing that is hidden from the eyesight of God. What's not view by people is always seen by God. Integrity shows how much you have grown over the years. It will let people know who you are a person. When you are of certain aged into adulthood, you know how to conduct yourself as a mature adult. The way you respond to situations whether the situation is good or bad you should always remain humble. Stay humble even when you are angry. Your character should never change outside of another person character because their problem upset you. Integrity is the love of God, and everything is not of Satan. Live your life in a place of integrity. God will always meet you there. God hears your cries, and He sees your pain. Your struggles are in the palm of his hand. He wakes you up every day and knows that you are trying to live your life the best way you know how. He directed you in the path of others whose words will encourage you not to give up. Even when you had all you can take, and wanted to end your life. God sent His Holy Spirit to your life to direct you into a brand new path. The way that God lead you to the streams of water that flow with the Spirit of Jesus. A way where people will help you gain your confidence. God says, "You are my child." When He hears your cries, He does what any Father would do when their child is in trouble. He will attend to His child, and He will make all the bad things go away. He will make everything in your life brand new. Always love the people who hate you, because of them God will keep blessing you. Happiness, Peace, and Joy with genuine love in your heart will keep good things coming to you. Be careful what you say, and keep good things coming from your mouth. This will always kill the enemy.

There are different stories in the bible that scripture unfolds some truths that we can learn from.

Look at this:

The story of the blind man in the Bible (King James Version)
(John 9:1-41)

There was a blind man, and he heard Jesus was coming through. The blind man Asked Jesus to lay hands on him and make him see again. Jesus told the man to close his eyes and wipe the blind man eyes with spit and dirt and healed the blind man, and now he can see again.

"And it came to pass, that as he came near unto Jericho, a certain blind man sat by the wayside begging."

(Luke 18:25)

God is Listening, and He Cares

When you think God isn't listening to your problems, He always has an open ear. He always has a concerning heart to help His children.

I shared this story with you to motivate you to believe that God has the power to heal anybody. There is power in the name of Jesus, to do all things known and unknown. If it were meant for you to be normal, you would have been born without disabilities, and complications. You have just to trust in the plan for your life, and God will see you through every single time. God sees your convictions in all of your struggles, and have admiration over all of it.

CHAPTER 8

Take Accountability For Your Actions

You now know there is a purpose for your life, and with that purpose there comes visions that God gives to you. You now have a full understanding of your disability. You should have enough wisdom to know that everyone isn't going to accept you for who you are, and many may come against you. The things people say shouldn't affect your ability to live your life. You have to build up enough confidence now to realize who you are, and what you can do. Knowing what you know now, you should become a person of integrity. We know what other people will do to you, but what do you do to people for them to mistreat you? Disabled people are often underestimated, because of their appearances. Some disabled people have an IQ of Albert Einstein, and they know right from wrong. They are acutely aware of what they are doing, and what's going on around them. Have you ever used your disability to get over on people? Have you ever used your disability to get what you want? Individuals with a disability sometimes think they are entitled to do whatever they want. They believe that society owes them something. Nobody owes you anything but respect. I know this for a fact because I am very smart, and I'm capable. I have knowledge of what's going on around me. I'm not paralyzed of learning and doing things on my own. Disabled people have boundaries to the things that they can and cannot do. Being disabled doesn't mean you can't do anything at all. Being disabled doesn't mean you are dumb. You are just limited to the things that are normal for someone else to do. You can't use your disability to get over on people because it wrong to do so. If no one ever told you this, please understand that getting what you want without the proper way of getting it, is called cheating. You are cheating yourself, and stealing the kindness of someone else's heart. You can't do it, and it's wrong. I believe some disabled people have the full potential of doing things, such as working, going to school, and handling their finances. Many of them have the potential of everyday living. I also believe that some disabled individuals take advantage of their disability to get away with things. It's bad enough that society criticizes us. You should carry yourself in a decent manner, and make yourself look like you are somebody. Don't be deceived as to what society makes you out to be. You are what you believe, and you are viewed on how you see yourself. Sometimes things that happen to us can are caused on our own for the lack of respect that we have for ourselves.

<u>Dealing with two words that are entirely different</u>

We have misused the word "disabled" and mistaken it for the word "handicap." The two terms have entirely different meanings but are unchangeably used as a clutch. It's very important to know the difference between the phrase to have full knowledge of who you are. Handicap slowdowns your progress while disabled enabled your psychological and physical abilities. God gave us all a mind with brains to help us to think. People with disabilities may not look like their brain isn't working, but in terms, they believe that how everyone else's thinks. They do things entirely different. A person with a handicap is capable of responding to what their mind is saying, but it may come off differently in the way you respond. Don't limit any consequences of punishment to a person with disabilities, because they need to know you cannot wrongfully do bad things and get away with it. Is it possible that disabled people that are handicap do not have self-control? Did anyone take the time to teach the young adult with disabilities how to have self- control? Self-control is a part of everyday living and should be taught at a young age. Parents, it's your responsibility to make sure your child have self-controlled because it's a part of their character. A child does not know what self- controlled is unless he or she is taught what it is. Can a child be born with self- Controlled? A child learns from the environment and the things that are around them. A child must be taught how to love and be kind to the right things around them and also be appreciative. Scriptures from the Bible teaches us about love, peace and joy and how to be kind bearing good fruits. The world made view your child as a child with disabilities, but God hath nourish the child, and His view is no different from how He see His children. Being born with a disability is no excuse, no reason not to have self-control. Having a disability without self-controlled is inexcusable nonsense to God. God grace is providing to give us the knowledge of what's right from wrong. When we do what's not of the will of God, then His grace is still given to us. His Grace is what keeps us, and holds us up. Disability does not give you the right to do whatever it is you want. You cannot be disobedient because you have a disability.

"But the fruit of the Spirit is love, joy, peace, patience, kindness, goodness, faithfulness, gentleness, and self-control. Against such thing, there is no law."

Galatians 5:22 -23

"For this very reason, make every effort to add to your faith goodness; and to goodness knowledge; and to knowledge, self-control; and to self-control, perseverance Godliness; and to Godliness brotherly kindness; and to brotherly kindness, love."

2 Peter 1:5-7

"But mark this: there will be terrible times in the last days. People will be lovers of themselves, lovers of money. Boastful, proud, abusive, disobedient to parents, ungrateful, unholy, without love, unforgiving, slanderous, without self-control, brutal, not lovers of the good."

2Timothy 3 1-3

When we take a look at what scripture says about self-control, we can see that it is very important for any child of God. I am a very smart individual who as accomplished a lot of my goals. I have Diplomas and certifications that I have earned over the years. I have my place and a bank account. I can manage my finances. All these things do not matter to me, and anyone that knows me. In other people's minds, they may think Terrell does not know what he is doing. God gave me the ability to know right from wrong. Anything I do whether it's good or bad, I am fully aware. I thought it first, then I planned it, and then I reacted to it. What I'm trying to get everyone to understand is that you can't put a limit on your disability. We must still be accountable for what's going on around us. Disabled people can be reliable, and there are some who will do what's right. I find it to be amusing and laugh how individuals with a title think they have such much power over people who are under them. If you are a leader of any sort, you are supposed to guide individuals who are for you to become the next leader in that position. We have too many dishonorable people in the church, and in this world. It makes non-believers not want to come to church or deal with society. Everyone will be held accountable for his or her actions. There are no exceptions as to who you are, and no one should be excused from being punished for a crime he or she have committed. Doctor, Lawyer, Mayor, Governor, Senator, or even President of the United States. If you commit a crime you will do time; you are not excused from punishment. Disabled people can be a Leader in a church, or in politics with a high position. Having a title in front of your name does not mean anything to God, especially if your heart is not right. Satan was once an angel, he was jealous and became wicked. God then kick Satan out of Heaven. Scripture tells us Satan took his tail and took some Angles down with him.

Falling Angels

These angels did not have the character of God, and was wicked and wanted to take over Heaven.

"For if God spared not the angels that sinned, but cast them down to hell, and delivered them into chains of darkness, to be reserved unto judgment."

2 Peter 2:4

Love

Love who you are without any regrets. You don't want to be disabled and have a mean heart. Then you won't be comfortable with your disability. You will be disabled and miserable. You will then hate your life because you have a mean heart. Disabled people can be loving people. They can be good people to lend a helping hand. Some show very high concern to others and are very protective when it comes to things that are important to them. Disabled people love to have fun and laugh. Don't be deceived everything that is sweet does not taste like honey. Love without Limits, and you will see that the life you live will be a happy one.

CHAPTER 9

Change Your Behavior

People will view you how you see yourself. People look at your appearance because it's the first thing people see when they see you. You must carry yourself in a respectable manner, always looking up to part. People can misinterpret one's character if you are not properly dressed or groomed. We must be able to correctly pronounce words, and communicate well for people to respect us. It is very important to try to use proper grammar to be able to talk right. When speaking to others it's always best to use good English, and do not use slang words. Always to give direct eye contact when talking to someone. We often assume we are aware of everything and know everything. We often believe everything that we're doing is right. Do we have that much pride that we are blind to our mistakes? Why can't we see what everyone else sees about us? Can we at least admit that there is something wrong with us, and try to fix it? America is so self-centered. We have no idea of the perception of knowing our self. You must have perception, and able to perceive things, and also be aware of what is going on around you. Personality, strengths, weaknesses, thoughts, beliefs, motivation, and emotions are one's character. If you can identify all of these things about yourself, then you have self-awareness. Self-awareness allows you to understand more about yourself and other people. Gained knowledge of what self-awareness is will better help you become aware of a lot of things. You will become more involve with yourself. It will bring a sense of awareness in your life. It will also bring a sense of knowing. It teaches you where you spend a lot of time, and motivates you to want to be more productive with your day. You must identify where you spend the most time.

Gary van Warmerdam states:

What do you focus on the most? Changing the interpretations in your mind allows you to change your emotions. Self-awareness is one of the attributes of Emotional Intelligence and an important factor in achieving success.

When you go for a checkup or an evaluation the doctor checks for things concerning 8 laboratory tests, and other diagnostic procedures. The physical examination should include: an appropriate measurement of BP, with verification in the contralateral arm; an examination of the optic fundi; a calculation of body mass index (BMI) (measurement of waist circumference is also very useful); an auscultation for carotid, abdominal, and femoral bruits; a palpation of the thyroid gland; a thorough examination of the heart and lungs; an examination of the abdomen for enlarged kidneys, masses, distended urinary bladder, and abnormal aortic pulsation; a palpation of the lower extremities for edema and pulses; and neurological assessment.

Evaluate

Evaluation is good for one's health, but when is the last time have you done a self-evaluation?

Business Dictionary.com defines self-evolution as:

Development and learning to determine what has improved and what areas still need improvement by looking at your progress. Usually, involves comparing a "before" situation with a current situation.

When you are self-evaluating yourself, you're analyzing yourself mentally physically and emotionally. What thoughts do you have about yourself? Have you made progress over the years? Are you just the same as you were last year? Maybe you haven't changed at all. Find the errors in your life then correct them. No one is perfect, we all have errors in our lives that need to be corrected. We all been through something similar, but in another form of direction. It's not the error we need to look at, but it's how we are going to change our lives around from the error.

Once you have identified what the problem that is in your life you must self-cleanse yourself spiritually from all the negative things that are harmful to you. Start by looking at the people that you surround yourself with on a daily basis.

Kristy Robinett said:

Some may call it bad luck, but it is actually negative energy that can cause life to turn upside down, or at least feel that way. Depression, fear, anger, arguments, psychic vampires (negative people), sadness, unhappiness, etc. clings like Saran Wrap to your aura field and attracts more of the same situations, along with exhaustion, fatigue, unhappiness, an unsettled feeling and sometimes even health conditions. Just as a furnace filter needs to be replaced or cleaned, so does your energy filter. How often you need to complete an energy cleanse dependent upon your personal and professional situation.

There are numerous ways that you can cleanse yourself, your office, your home and even your car. Anywhere that you spend your time is fair game to have residual energy, good and bad energy, attach to you.

Ways to Cleanse Yourself

Get rid of all the negativity in, and around you. You have to step up and make the change. No one else will do it for you.

Spiritual Leader

The best way to do a spiritual cleanse is to have a pastor or a deacon, elder whomever in the church that you feel comfortable to pray with you.

Things that harm us and make us become bitter as a person these things are poisons to our lives.

Anger
Hate
Loss
Negativity

Do you need to remove some things out of your life to live a peaceful life?

You can be angry when things don't go your way. You can also get angry when something or someone upset you.

I don't like feeling angry because I may do or say something I don't mean. Being angry cause me not to eat or sleep.

Having a strong dislike of something or someone is called hate.

Always have love within your heart, hate can cause you to be disliked by God. Please understand that hate isn't a feeling God created. God is love, and not hate.

Life Happens

We can become attached to things that may become hard for use to let go out our lives. When holding on to money, family, clothes, shoes, even our job is affecting our lives in so many ways. We get so hooked on these things, and we lose focus on things that matter. Materialistic things will pass away; you can lose it anytime. When we lose these things, we tend to have an emotional breakdown and feel that we can't live anymore. A loss is something that happens.

<u>Stay Away from Negative People</u>

Stay away from negative habits or people who influence you to do things that you don't feel comfortable with. If you're not comfortable with something, leave it alone, and don't look back at it.

Use prudence against the things that folly fools you.

Once you have identified what the problem is that you are having in your life, then fix them. A lot of problems can be fixed. Once you know what the negativity things that are harming you, fix them fast. Correct the negative things so that you will be able to live a more productive life. You must have self- discipline, and correct all the things that are wrong in your life. With self-discipline, it helps you to understand better what is right and wrong for you.

Iowa states:

DEVELOPING SELF-DISCIPLINE

Self-discipline
Self-discipline can be considered a type of selective training, creating new habits of thought, action, and speech toward improving yourself and reaching goals. Self-discipline can also be task oriented and selective. View self-discipline as positive effort, rather than one of denial.

Advantage: When you have a clear idea as to what you want to achieve for the day at its start, the chances are very high that you will be able to accomplish the tasks proactively. Writing or sketching out the day helps.

Discouragement:

- Do not be intimidated; do not be put off by the challenge
- If you slip, remember this is natural
- Take a break and then refresh the challenge

Role models:

Observe the people in your life and see to what extent self-discipline and habits help them accomplish goals. Ask them for advice on what works, what doesn't.

<u>Live A Life That Is Pleasing</u>

We live in a world that is full of sin. Sin can lead you to fall into divers temptations. These temptations can harm your lives if you are not careful. We can harm those around us, and those who are a part of our lives if we are not careful. When you have a bad personality, it pushes people away from you, and they don't want to be bothered with you. You can have bad energy that comes from you, and even you won't be able to identify it. Others know when they are around someone who is negative, and they never have anything good to say about others. The people around you can feel your vibe. A person that gives off peace, love, and happiness can be quickly identified. You have to know within yourself that you want to change; nothing changes unless you allowed it to change. Self –Awareness, self-Cleanses, and self-Discipline will help make a lot of changes in your life. Don't be naïve to your self-pity. You are better than whom people view you as.

"Ye are of God, little children, and have overcome them: because greater is he that is in you than he that is in the world."

(1 John 4:4)

You are a child of God, and there should be nothing negative about you. You are the light, and you should let that light shine so others can be able to see it and feel it. Connecting to God will help you be positive, and it will help you make the changes you need in life. As Children of God we are above, and not beneath.

CHAPTER 10

An Open Letter For You

I haven't been a lot of places, but I've always seen the sun rise. I haven't experienced a lot of tragedies, but I've made it through the storm. I haven't been to war, but I had to fight for peace within myself. I haven't died, but I haven't lived until God said it's all done. People may never like what I do. People may never compliment me on the good things that I've achieved. People will always ignore me when I walk by, but I will always smile. I can't change what have already been done. I can't plan what God has already planned for me to do, but I can give you an open idea of what I have always felt in my heart. I have a disability but, I haven't lived the life as a person with a disability. I will never live my life not being able to express myself. I'm an independent person, and if I can't be independent, then I wouldn't be myself. Disabilities do not hurt my feelings, nor does it affect whom I was called to be. Disabilities don't define who you are and shouldn't affect you. I have done so much in my life that sometimes I have forgotten that I have a disability. I live my life in the form of a disabled person. God have allowed me to go through what disabled people go through so that I can be able to help someone else. I'm just a disabled young adult, who's allowing my life to be used as a testimony. This testimony will help the next disabled person through every situation in their lives. God wants me to share some light with you. Please stop downing yourself, because you are greater than what people think you are. Your life serves a purpose; there is nothing God created that doesn't. Everything that God Created has to mean. Being disabled is just the same as a person who is sick.

Being disabled is the same as a person who is poor or a person who is homeless. It's all the same type of struggle, but a different situation. I never understood why my life had to be in this way, so I began to ask God Why?

Lord why me?

How come God?

I had to learn how to trust God even during the times I didn't understand. It wasn't my time to understand what God plan for my life was going to be. In the midst of it all, I had to trust Him. while living my life as a disabled person, living life with so many unanswered questions. I don't know too much about where I came from, but I only know what was told to me. I don't know if what I was told was a lie or not. The evidence shows because the doctor has given me the name "Cerebral Palsy." If you were to look up and define what that word means, then take a look at me, then you will see that I don't look like what the meaning implies. You are looking at who I am in the physical. That's where the doctors made their mistakes when they misdiagnosed me.

What Causes Cerebral Palsy?

WebMD: Better information. Better health websites states:

Congenital cerebral palsy results from brain injury during a baby's development in the womb. It is present at birth, although it may not be detected for months. It is responsible for CP in about 70% of the children who have it. An additional 20% are diagnosed with congenital cerebral palsy due to a brain injury during the birthing process. In most cases, the cause of congenital cerebral palsy is unknown. Some possible causes are:

Infections during pregnancy that may damage a fetus' developing nervous system. These include rubella (German measles), cytomegalovirus (a herpes-type virus), and toxoplasmosis (an infection caused by a parasite that can be carried in cat feces or inadequately cooked meat). Other infections in pregnant women that may go undetected are being recognized now as an important cause of developmental brain damage in the fetus.

Palsies" -- disorders that impair control of movement due to damage to the developing brain. CP usually develops by age 2 or 3 and is a no progressive brain disorder, meaning the brain damage does not continue to worsen throughout life. However, the symptoms due to the brain damage often change over time -- sometimes getting better and sometimes getting worse. CP is one of the most common causes of chronic childhood disability.

Truth Be Told

God had covered me when I was a fetus; He blocked every drug that was supposed to do harm to my body. If Cerebral Palsy is a brain disease, my faith in God healed me, and my brain was never affected. I stand on His word. His word states:

"I can do all things through Christ which Strengthen me."

Philippians 4: 13

Living by that kept my faith in God alive. It has allowed me to work towards my ability to do whatever it is I have a heart desire to do. Everything that I say or I do always include God. Everything that my life is about is because of God. I believe He has called me to do great things. I have not answered to any other name but "Greatness." Greatness is who I am through Christ Jesus. Palsy I am not. What I love about God is that He never let us down. He lives within me. I want to thank all of you who came up against me. You all may have thought that I would fail by now, but I haven't. Every gift and talent that I have are because of you. When you said it's wasn't possible for me to do, God said," I have given you the ability to do it, Terrell." The voice of God said," When people say you have Cerebral Palsy, I say you do not have Cerebral Palsy."

I would never forget the day; I asked my mom about being adopted. It was the day of the Michael Jackson trial on June 13, 2005. I was hurt and angry at the same time. I wasn't thinking about how to approach the situation, and I asked her out of anger. The way I asked, and approached her was wrong, and it upset my Mother.

I've dealt with a lot of depression that medication could never fix. I just wanted to be loved. Everybody treated me differently, and I wanted to be treated like everyone else was treated. They viewed me as a person with disabilities. I still had a loving heart. I really never questioned where I came from until the age 16. I didn't realize how asking questions could cause harm, but it did.

Parents

I understand you as a parent with adopted children are hurt. Children and teens have feelings too. They hurt just like anyone else. Parents you say it's better not knowing than knowing at all.

Children/Adults

If you were adopted and raised with a family since birth, you might want to know the history. Years down the road, you may want a lot of questions answered. You are not wrong for asking questions because you deserve to know. Be careful of the way in which you ask questions. Asking questions should be done the right way, and in the appropriate manner, don't be disrespectful.

I Wanted To Know

When you want to know something, you just have to learn to ask. I'm smarter now to know that a lot of questions, can hurt people if not asked appropriately.

I asked questions like:

Why didn't you tell me I was adopted?

Who is my birth mother?

My questions weren't wrong, but I had to make sure that I used the appropriate approach. I needed to make sure my tone was right, and that I wasn't disrespectful in any way.

My mother wasn't answering me, but I kept asking. Eventually, she finally gave me some details. Your mother used drugs, and she was drinking a lot while she was pregnant with you. She also tried to sell you for a bottle of liquor. I was hurt because my mother was hurt. I may have come off as disrespectful, but I wanted to know. I needed to stop looking at the situation in a negative way. This day was a day that I could remember so well. She answered all my questions, but with tears in her eyes. Truthfully, secrets that are kept can destroy lives. Not knowing can save you from being hurt. Sadness can turn into bitterness. Through that bitterness, things can be said that shouldn't be said. It is good that I have a relationship with God. I knew the word of God at a young age, and still, know the word of God today. Even though I know the Lord, I still have a lot to learn. Although the situation turned out bad, I still love my mother.

A Prayer for Mom

This was my prayer every single night.

"Lord please give my mother and me a better relationship, because you said in your word to Honor your mother and father. So please forgive me on how I treated her."

Prayer works, and I never stopped praying. I continued to pray, and trust God. She had made the statement before she passed in a conversation with my siblings that, "Terrell have changed a lot." A lot of that anger didn't come from my mother; she was all about peace. A lot of the anger came from her husband. Some men have the attitude of not caring because they feel like they don't have to. Especially, if they are living with younger people that are not their kids. He was the type that only tolerated me, because of my mother. He was that type of guy. I wanted to get away from all of that negativity. I wanted to make a change for myself. I knew if I didn't get away things would've gotten worst, and I didn't want to stress my mother out.

A Change

I avoided all of that and went to Job Corps; then I went off to college afterward. My life living here in High Point, North Carolina was not a choice. When you think small, you do things that are small, and you receive things that are small. High Point is a very small area. I've lived here for two years; I moved here in 2013 with an ex-friend of mine. I've lived in two apartments which the first one my ex-friend and I shared. I haven't met any new friends other than my church family. Living here is very hard because I have no family nor friends here who can help me out. I attend church here in High Point. My Church name is "Monument of Praise." I love my pastor and church family. I would like to grow closer to God, and see new things happen within my life. I have made lots of mistakes since I've been living here, some which I am not proud of. I'm learning to become better within in myself. Every day's a new opportunity to learn new things, correct mistakes, and live life with new choices. Cerebral Palsy I'm am not.

I dislike people who are always in the judgment of other people's lives especially mine. People who are judgmental are all uneducated, you all refuse to learn about disabled people. You don't have an understanding of a disabled person, and the sad thing is you don't want to learn about a disabled person. In fact, you are so busy focusing on what we can and cannot do. I don't think you have an idea of your life. We have the ability to do all things through Christ. We are smart, brilliant, and regular individuals. God made this world, and who are you to judge. Love haven't been a committed thing in my life. Love is not something that you act on love is something that you do. People can love you for materialistic things, and money. I know some of you don't care about my wellbeing. There are some who are waiting for the day that they can get on social media to see R.I.P by my name. I deal with people who say they're my friends if it weren't for fear of loneliness I wouldn't consider you as one.

The nation is filled with envy and hate. Americans have so much jealousy in their hearts, then other people from others cultures. We can point the finger at someone else when we're struggling just like the next person. Love isn't real until people enter your life, and have experienced your situations and pray genuinely for you. Once they know what you are going through, they will pray that God will bring you out of your situation. When God have blessed your life the people who say they love you won't hate you, because of the things God works out for you. If those people genuinely love you, they will celebrate what God has done for you. I've opened up too many people about my disability and having HIV, but only one have opened back up to me. With being rejected for so many years. I forgot that the devil could come in disguised because he once was an angel If are a person with a disability and you are desperate for love, and you are willing to open up your heart to someone, just make sure the person will Experience, Pray, and celebrate everything you are going through. I don't like being rejected but if living alone will direct and protect me from the venom and the poisons of your heart, I will live alone until the day I died. Please don't cry at my funeral or speak over my body. I thank God for what he allowed my life to be because I would have had another story to tell. Being disabled have given me a passionate heart for disabled people. Disability has become my ministry. I know how you feel. I cried the same tears. I have gotten the same look. I have been marked. You are not in this alone. I will be with you here now and forever. I'm much better than I've ever been while going through this journey of being disabled. I will be the voice in your ear to encourage you to move on. I will be the love in your heart. My spirit will forever live in each and every one of you. Thank you to all of you who are disabled to allow me to be an encouragement to your life. I pray something I've had said will help you to live your life in a new way. Opening up to the world was never about me. I've opened up to be a blessing to all of you. My heart's desire is that you are delivered and that you reach the next level in your life. I pray for you and hope that you see life in a totally different way now. Have I accomplished that goal? I have shared some personal information about my personal and sex life. I know there will be fire thrown at me, but when you are growing in God, you will have to face this. You will have to bare crucifixion like Jesus did when he died on the cross. I know there will be many questions asked on when and how? Let me ask you this before you question me on my life. Have you live an innocent life without making any mistakes, or have you always been successful?

Remember this:

"Everyone suffers before getting to the Promise Land."
May God Bless You and Heaven Smile Upon You!!!!!!!!!!!!!!!!!!!!

MEET THE AUTHOR

Author Terrell Scott

Praise the Lord Everybody,

Hello, my name is Terrell Scott, I currently reside in High Point NC, but I'm from Bronx, New York. I grew up in South Carolina, and I am a graduate of Sumter High School. I completed Office Administration at Bamberg Job Corps Center in Bamberg, S.C. I also obtained a career diploma in Introduction to Psychology from Ashworth College in North Cross, GA. Hidden underneath all of my accomplishments, I am a former special education student. My Mother died when I was at the age of 24, and that day shifted my entire life. I am the third oldest of  four children. I enjoy going different places and learning new things. You have never seen the world until you have traveled around the world. I am a member at Monument of Praise in High Point, NC where I reside I love going to church. I am a writer of emotions, and my best work comes pouring out of me whether I'm happy, sad or even angry. I have written a lot of poetry that is unpublished, "Palsy I Am Not" is my first book. My goal is to reach people of all ages. I have great compassion for disabled people because I have been identified as one for many years. I came in contact with drugs as a fetus in my mother's womb, I've endured so much negativity, and have been judged by many. People have prejudged me before even getting to know me. The sad thing is people haven't tried to get to know me, and never wanted to know the person that I am. I've been rejected, talked about, manipulated, used, and abused. The last thing my mother said to me, and I will never forget it. She said, "Stop letting people use and abuse you; I raised you better than that." I like shopping for new things, but if I don't have something I just don't have it. I also enjoy going out to eat. I love trying new foods. I was delayed in accomplishing many of my goals, and my dreams, because I didn't have the proper support I needed to make those dreams come true. In God there is no failure, I had to trust and rely on Him to get me to where I am today. I have many hidden talents that God himself did not reveal to me. One thing I do know if I haven't learned anything else throughout this Journey in my life is that my life has been nothing more than a testimony. It has been a testimony to deliver people of all ages, sickness, and disabilities to help them prosper in their lives, and live out God's divine purpose. I hope that you have enjoyed reading this book because I enjoyed every moment pouring out my heart to see others set free, and delivered.

Notes

Maya Angelou Quotes

http://www.goodreads.com/

Gary van Warmerdam
http://www.pathwaytohappiness.com/about_gary_background.htm

Patient Evaluation - The Seventh Report of the
Joint National Committee on Preve...

Kristy Robinett

http://www.patheos.com/blogs/ahappymedium/2012/06/
re-aligning-your-spirit-removing-negativity-energy/

Mahanthi Bukkapaptnam

http://www.studygs.net/discipline.htm

Cerebral Palsy
http://www.webmd.com/brain/
understanding-cerebral-palsy-basic-information#0

All Bible verses are in quotations, came from
King James Version of The Bible.
King James Version of the Bible

Printed in the United States
By Bookmasters